DURAN DURAN
Their story

✸ **K**ASPER *de* **G**RAAF &
✸ **M**ALCOLM **G**ARRETT

Kasper de Graaf first interviewed **D**uran **D**uran when working for *Smash Hits*, before the band released their debut single 'Planet Earth'. He has stayed in contact with them throughout their hectic rise to fame, both as a friend and as editor of *New Sounds New Styles*, a monthly magazine that appeared between March 1981 and July 1982.

Malcolm Garrett started working with **D**uran **D**uran as their graphic designer when they signed to EMI Records and has designed all their record sleeves and publicity material. He was design director for *New Sounds New Styles* and with his design team *Assorted iMaGes*, he has provided the packaging for many bands including Simple Minds, Buzzcocks and Magazine. Much of this work was featured in the touring *Cover Versions* exhibition in 1981.

Editor (Publishing) Chris Goodwin
Typeset in Bodoni by SX Composing
Additional setting by Focus Photoset
Reproduction by Aragorn
Printed & bound in the UK by Cook, Hammond & Kell Limited

First published in UK *1982*
First published in USA *1983*

Photographers: Peter Ashworth, Mark Babushkin, Joe Bangay, Neil Bicknell, Nancy Campbell, Fin Costello, Andy Earl, Paul Edmond, Frank Griffin, Steve Hickey, Gered Mankowitz, Nick Rhodes, Andy Taylor, John Taylor, Andy Warhol, Eric Watson, Larry Williams *et al.*

Proteus Books is an imprint of the Proteus Publishing Group.

United States
Proteus Publishing Co. Inc.
9 West *57*th Street, Suite *4504*
New York, N.Y. *10019*

distributed by
The Scribner Book Companies Inc.
597 Fifth Avenue
New York, N.Y. *10017*

United Kingdom
Proteus (Publishing) Limited
Bremar House
Sale Place
London W*2 1*PT

ISBN *0 86276 171 9* (paperback)

Nick: *"John and I were having a lunchtime drink in the Hole in The Wall [a Birmingham city centre pub], trying to decide a name. We'd been through everything. We'd been through books, film titles, we'd looked on walls and in the dictionary. We'd made up words and everything a band usually does. There is one name I remember – RAF. It didn't stand for anything, we just liked it.*

"Then the film Barbarella *came up in conversation and I think it was John that said, Duran Duran, that doesn't sound bad! What about that for a name? And there it was."*

In punkdrenched '78, an interesting figure was cut by that first group of Nick Rhodes (Wasp synth and rhythm unit), John Taylor (then lead guitar), Steve Duffy (vocals and occasional bass) who as TinTin recently signed his own contract with WEA, and a guy called Simon Colley, who played bass and doubled on clarinet. The band played its first gig together with an early incarnation of Fashion at a club appropriately named Barbarellas, then very much the centre of the Birmingham scene. Their sound was not unlike that of Soft Cell's recent 'What' 12-inch.

Nick was 16 and had just left school. Born Nicholas James Bates (the Rhodes came later) on June 8th 1962 in Birmingham, his very earliest memory is mixing up stones with his mum's potatoes – *"it was probably about the first time anybody realised just how important Freud was in life."* His schooling appears by and large to have been an irrelevant episode. On the very first day *"there was this classroom full of kids and I had to sit down and listen to this rather tall, skinny, almost ugly, screaming dragon teach a bunch of idiots and me how to read and write. Of course, I found this rather distressing at such a tender age."*

Distress had turned to disinterest by the time he reached the third year of secondary school. Although he never minded school that much, he figured then that he wasn't learning anything except how to pass exams – and he didn't exactly set much store by those:

"I swore when I left school that I was never gonna use any of my O-levels or anything, ever. I knew they were entirely useless to me. The main thing I learned at school, which was invaluable to me later on, was about people and psychology."

While Nick was busy getting born in or around Moseley, the Taylor household less than a mile away was preparing for the second birthday of its only child almost a fortnight hence. John Nigel Taylor (at that time it was actually Nigel John but it was "changed for, er, aesthetic reasons, as David Sylvian once said in *Sounds*") had been born on June 20th 1960. His father was employed at a car components factory, his mother worked part-time at a school and he was raised in the house he still lives in with his parents today. A bright and promising start at Roman Catholic primary school quickly evaporated when at the age of 14, two years into the County High School, he decided that reading the *New Musical Express* was more fruitful, or at any rate more palatable, than going to history lessons.

From then on, even though he couldn't play a note, he knew that one way or another, he "had to get into it". A final effort to turn his academically minded school to advantage by asking the music teacher for guitar lessons drew the icy response that only proper orchestra instruments were taught, and even a characteristic JT compromise suggestion that he learn to play the saxophone fell on tone-deaf ears. Although now he wishes he'd learned to play the piano and paid more attention in language classes, he ended up thinking that school had nothing to offer him:

"*It was just, at the time, I'd be sitting there looking at bloody logarithms and I'd think, well, what's the point of this? I wish they'd teach me to drive instead.*"

John went in for his A-levels but failed them all for lack of incentive: he'd already been accepted into art college on the strength of his folio. It was around this time that Nick and John combined their creative talents to swim an elegant backstroke against the tidal wave of punk. Their heroes were people like Bryan Ferry, David Bowie and Rod Stewart; they wore make-up and dressed UP, not down.

With hindsight their progress may seem inevitable, but in those early days it was far from certain; their musical identity was still embryonic, smooth and inspired management was well beyond their dreams and there was no well-defined purpose among the members of *Duran Duran* Mark I.

John did a year's foundation course at art college and gained top marks for his first end-of-term display:

"*Actually, I used a lot of early Duran Duran posters. I did the whole thing on black plastic and just only used red, black and white, cos I was on a red, black and white trip at the time. You know, I've always been into that, the Russian constructivist thing, and I just used those colours all the way through and they loved it. Well, I thought, we're well away here . . .*"

But the rebellion against academic discipline soon resurfaced and his final end-of-year presentation consisted of nothing but the very first *Duran Duran* demo tape:

"*I suppose I was testing them up to a point, because art college teachers think they're so progressive. But when you say to them, look, I've created this out of nothing –*

Auntie Linda's wedding. Nick (second from left) proves that he was into frilly shirts well before his time.

"John! That's it! I'll change my name to John!"

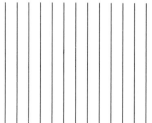

isn't this the same as writing on paper? – they don't quite know how to handle it. But they had to give me the benefit of the doubt and just about pass me for the course."

2

Although many musicians came and went, there were really only four serious incarnations of *Duran Duran*. Original members Steve Duffy and Simon Colley left because they wanted to go more rock 'n' roll. Undeterred, Nick and John recruited Andy Wickett who until then had been singer with one of their favourite bands, TV Eye (a sort of Birmingham equivalent of the New York Dolls), and who "wanted to get into something a little bit more conceptual". This lineup showed the earliest traces of the present *Duran Duran* sound. John or Nick ("We'll argue about it till the cows come home so there's no point," says John) came up with the chorus for 'Girls On Film', which remained more or less intact with each singer writing a different song around it until the Simon le Bon version appeared on the first album.

As the band improved, the need to tighten up the sound led to the next major development: the recruitment of Roger Taylor.

Nick: *My rhythm unit only had rumba, foxtrot, slow rock, fast rock and swing on it, so we decided that we needed a drummer to compensate. Andy Wickett got drunk one night at a party and approached this James Dean lookalike, Roger Taylor, who was once a member of the hideously titled Birmingham combo Crucified Toad but was currently playing in the semilegendary Scent Organs. Fortunately Andy had noticed the young lad's skin-bashing potential and had the cheek to invite our Rodge down to a rehearsal. The next day . . . no, that day, he joined. And things have been downhill ever since.*"

In reality, Roger Andrew Taylor was just the sort of fastidious and skilled musician needed to give *Duran Duran* a solid backbone. A couple of months older than John, he was born on April 26th 1960 in Castle Bromwich, where he still lives with his parents. He became passionately interested in music at about the age of ten and the first band he went to see was The Jackson Five. He copied his elder brother, a Tamla

Motown fan, and used to listen to his records. When he was about 15, he began buying Genesis records. Still at school, he started putting bands together with his friends and at 17, he played his first gig with a punk outfit in a Birmingham club.

When he first met Nick and John they found a common interest in certain post-punk bands, like The Cure and Siouxsie, though at that time, he says, "John and Nick were a bit more funky . . . I got into that through John." John recalls being impressed by Roger "being good in a Rat Scabies sort of way, i.e. hit as many drums as possible in a tenth of a second. He was the only one in Birmingham who could keep up with Nick's Wasp going, *'deet-deet-deet-deet-deet-deet-deet tzunda tzunda tzunda dada dada'* . . ." Roger joined Andy Wickett, Nick and John to make the very first **Duran Duran** demo tape (including 'Girls On Film') with producer-about-Brum Bob Lamb of UB40 fame, John playing both guitar and bass.

Andy Wickett left and a new singer was needed. Meanwhile, a hardcore **Duran Duran** sound was beginning to develop around the nucleus of Nick, Roger and John, an important factor being the latter's switch from lead guitar to bass:

"I'd started to play the guitar because all my heroes were guitarists. I never listened to the bass at all, was never aware of it. I always fancied myself as Johnny Thunders or Mick Ronson – you know, someone that takes the flash, comes forward in the spotlight. Bernard Edwards was the first bass player that I ever listened to and that was the first time that I actually realised that the bass player really does guide the tune. So then I got out my old Roxy records and started listening to the bass. Then there was the excitement of hearing Roger play. We'd never had a drummer before and I really wanted to play with him so I was going half and half. We'd say, well, let's try this one number and play bass with him and then we'd play another number – this is in rehearsals – playing guitar. And I just settled in, I felt so comfortable playing with Rodge; it was just a natural decision really.".

A "Modern guitarist for Roxy/Bowie influenced band" ad persuaded Londoner Alan Curtis to join and this third line-up was completed by Jeff Thomas, a John Foxx-inspired singer previously with Roger's old band The Scent Organs.

Duran Duran were pulling themselves out of the lethargy of talking rather than doing, of wavering about what to do next. Their direction began to click with that new, tight disco rhythm section. Rehearsing in a squat in Cheapside, just off Birmingham's industrial Bradford Street, they found inspiration in Chic and in records like Rod Stewart's 'Do Ya Think I'm Sexy', 'Miss You' by the Rolling Stones, Bowie's 'Young Americans' album and some of Giorgio Moroder's collaborative projects, most notably with Sparks and Donna Summer. Some key ingredients were still missing, but the determination to find them was there.

It's a deal! **Duran Duran** soon after signing to EMI Records, January *1981*.

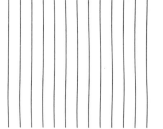

Towards the turn of the decade, Britain's disco scene was still in the greasy grip of Fever, throttled by the Bee Gees. Music from the Midlands equalled reggae and ska, with bands like Steel Pulse, UB40, The Beat and The Specials. Bryan Ferry had faded temporarily into the background. Kraftwerk and their dummies were hiding out in the seclusion of their Kling Klang studio; electronics meant Gary Numan.

In New York, a less bland and much more powerful disco scene was centred on clubs like Studio 54. Two visitors from England, brothers Paul and Michael Berrow, were taking a close and careful look and deciding to attempt the seemingly impossible feat of importing the Studio 54/Xenon scene back to the club they'd bought in Birmingham.

Back home they did up the club – the Rum Runner in Broad Street, close to the city centre – organised Bowie/Roxy nights and jazz funk nights, and ran a tight music policy strongly inspired by New York's Chic powerdisco.

Legend has it that **Duran Duran** walked into the Rum Runner one day with a tape and walked out again with a pot of gold and a glamorous future signed on the dotted line, but the truth is more prosaic. The band needed venues for gigs and Nick and John took in a tape containing four tracks, one of which was 'Girls On Film' and one that was later to be the basis for 'Late Bar'. Already impressed by the club's music policy, they now found that the owners were on a very similar wavelength to their own. "They were looking for a band that was a cross between Gino Soccio, Genesis and Chic," remembers Roger. The appeal was mutual and the Berrows offered rehearsal space and gigs, but it was still quite a few months and a lot of hard work before a management deal was signed.

Guitarist Alan Curtis and singer Jeff Thomas soon departed for more barren pastures. Nick, Roger and John were now developing such a locked-on idea of what they wanted that recruiting the rest of the line-up became a lengthy and demanding process. They auditioned dozens of singers and guitarists, trying out a fair few as members of the band along the way. They made strenuous efforts to contact ex-Rich Kids guitarist Steve New, but when their messages and telegrams remained unanswered, decided he wouldn't be the right person anyway.

They placed ads in the music press.

Michael and Paul Berrow. Rum Runner office, January *1981*.

Simon le Bon – vocals

John Taylor – bass guitar

Roger Taylor – drums

Nick Rhodes – keyboards

Andy Taylor – lead guitar

Several hundred miles away on Tyneside, restless rocker Andy Taylor had been hopping from band to band every few months looking for an outfit that shared his professional enthusiasm and determination. He was an experienced guitarist, having served his time with a variety of pop groups and travelled most of Europe, at one time living in Germany for 13 months. Now he scanned his *Melody Maker* and found a likely ad for a guitarist in a Birmingham band. He phoned to arrange an audition, collected all his worldly goods to exchange for a rail ticket and one Friday, jumped on the train with his guitar and Marshall combo.

Andrew Taylor (his full name today is Andrew Wilson-Taylor since his marriage in July 1982 to Tracey Wilson) was born at Tynemouth Royal Infirmary – about nine miles from Newcastle – on February 16th 1961. His father was a fisherman and so was his grandfather, who used to live above them in the tiny fishing village of Cullercoats. His is the most genuine Duran sob story: they had an outside toilet and a tin bath and money was in desperately short supply.

Expectations that Andy might follow his father and grandfather to sea were dashed at an early stage when the decline in the fishing industry forced his father into carpentry. Andy played a lot of football and did well at school, passing his eleven plus and going to grammar school.

"And the first day I went to grammar school – dead exciting, you know – well, I came home and me mother had gone! So I thought, oh well, it's just me and me old man and me little brother . . ."

After some time the family moved and Andy transferred to comprehensive school, where the syllabus was so far behind that of his former school that he lost all interest. He started messing around in a band and played his first gig when he was 13.

"I totally lost interest in school, become a real bum and drop-out, never used to go at all. And then I became the black sheep kid at school cos I had long hair and played in groups, and all the rest of the lads were going camping or something . . . I wasn't into that. And then the black sheep of the family – 'oooh, can you make a living doing that?'"

Well-intentioned efforts on the part of careers teachers to push Andy into a solid trade like bricklaying, plumbing or stonemasonry all fell on deaf ears. Although too young to leave school, he simply stopped going and devoted himself completely to music. None of the bands he was in were really capable of writing songs and developing a style successfully, but they would play other people's songs and try to do them as well as possible. It was good training and he persisted despite the problems it caused:

"I got into all sorts of trouble at school. But when your heart's in something, you just do it. I didn't even think about it really."

The train arrived in Birmingham. Andy jumped out and wandered round the city looking for the Rum Runner. When he got there, Nick, John and Roger were jamming in the upstairs bar, waiting for yet another guitarist.

"And they were like, the biggest bunch of weirdos that I'd ever seen. Which turned us on straight away, cos I'd always felt like being weird, but I had no-one to be weird with in Newcastle. You know, it's that sort of thing . . . It's not just about playing, there's a whole spirit of forming a band and a style and there was all that incorporated when I met them, not just playing the music. But then they had this chorus for a song that went – Girls On Film, Girls On Film, and I thought, hell, that's good. You know, the rest of it, there was nothing, it was the only bit that was there before the five of us got together and started writing the songs. And I just thought that'd be a hit, you know. And then the attraction was quite quick. Nick didn't like us cos I had jeans on. Roger and John did. John just thought I was the best player that he'd ever seen and played with. Fitting into a band takes time, but the spirit was right and [it was] just what I felt I wanted to do."

He must have communicated this feeling quite forcefully to Nick, who recalls:

"Andy came down from Newcastle to Birmingham for an audition and he was such a noisy sod and he had such a big mouth and pushed things so much that he threatened us we'd fall apart if he didn't join. So he pressurised us into allowing him to play guitar."

The day before, John had been listening to Gary Moore's album 'Back On The Streets' and was very conscious of the fact that this was the sort of broad range of guitar playing that was required, with some tracks of almost Thin Lizzyesque rock and others very funky, like Weather Report. Asked at the audition who his favourite guitarist was, Andy replied Gary Moore. That, and a practical demonstration, was enough for John.

Roger remembers that Andy "was more like Johnny Thunders – different". **Duran Duran** wanted power and sensitivity; Andy Taylor had plenty of both.

The Berrows were looking after them as they worked hard developing their identity. They bought John a new bass guitar and Nick a synthesiser – the first that wasn't a Wasp. It wasn't much compared to the large amounts involved today in the **Duran Duran** enterprise, but in those days it was a big step forward from rehearsing in a squat with what they could find. Andy, who had come to Birmingham without anywhere to live, slept on settees at Nick's or the Berrows or *"with all sorts of people that I'll not mention now that I'm married."*

They had to earn their keep. Andy painted the walls at the Rum Runner, John polished the mirrors, Roger retained his daytime job in a factory. Nick, always a more leisured creature, did his bit as DJ:

"I used to be quite good at mixing. I always remember that 'John I'm Only Dancing' frizzled out very well into a mix of 'Both Ends Burning'. What I used to like doing was filling the dance floor with three really popular songs, and then putting something else on that none of them knew, and it was so packed they couldn't move so they had to dance to it. And that's the way of breaking records in clubs."

But still they didn't have a singer.

Nick: *"Ah . . . yes! Well of course, we didn't tell Andy this when he joined . . . So when he arrived at the first rehearsal with his guitar slung over one shoulder and his Marshall over the other he said, well, where's the singer? Oh, he's not here today, he's on holiday. But we're gonna try some new ones out."*

And this is where Fiona Kemp came in.

Simon le Bon became a pop singer courtesy of a theatrically inclined mum, a choirmaster named Turvey and an ex-girlfriend who was a barmaid in the right place at the right time.

Born Simon John Charles le Bon (known as Charley to the rest of the band, he and Roger are the only members of **Duran Duran** whose name has not undergone some change since it was first registered) on October 27th 1958 at Bushey Maternity Hospital near Watford, Herts, he was the first of three sons in a family descended from the Huguenots – French Protestants who escaped from Catholic France in the 16th and 17th centuries. The family originally came from Normandy. Simon's auntie says that their coat of arms can be found on the Huguenot crypt in Canterbury Cathedral.

Simon's earliest memory is of little coloured things in front of his face in the pram:

"I can remember playing with these things in front of my face, on something springy, like elastic or something; string. I can remember being in a pushchair and going over this hard, pebbly, concrete road and going 'aaa-aaa-aaa-aaa' and it would sound all shakey because of the hard wheels of the pushchair."

Such carefree bliss was not destined to last. Simon's mother, whose own performing ambitions were restricted by marriage, transferred them to little Simon by enrolling him for acting classes twice a week after school from about the age of five. He stayed with it for 12 years, becoming interested in Shakespeare and going to festivals, winning occasional medals and cups for poetry.

Mr. Turvey, the choirmaster at Pinner Parish Church and a determined man, put a hymnbook in Simon's hands during his latter years at primary school and coached him to sing. He became good at it, frequently singing treble solos, and eventually cutting his very first record with the choir, singing old church songs.

By 1977 he'd got the bug and set up a punk band that eventually settled on the name Dog Days. They rehearsed for absolutely ages and played their one and only set at Harrow Tech at the end of the Summer Term 1978:

"It was great. We were bottom of the bill underneath Supercharge, a band called 98th Precinct and some other art school band. We played actually on the floor, they wouldn't even put us on the stage. So there was like the bubble of the audience around us, and we got turned off because we went on for too long. They pulled my mike out and I went over to somebody else's, it was really funny. And after we went, everybody else went home or met us down the pub later on. Didn't stay and see Supercharge – strange but true . . ."

Simon failed most of his A-levels at sixth form college and by 1979 he was working in a hospital and doing an extra A-level at night school. He applied to Birmingham University for a drama course and got in. Sometime during that first and only year at University, he had a girlfriend called Fiona Kemp.

By the summer term, Simon felt increasingly that he wanted to *do* something, although he was by no means certain what. Fiona, a barmaid at the Rum Runner, knew that **Duran Duran** were looking for a singer and suggested it to him. "So I thought, well, why not? Why not for the summer?" He phoned up, spoke to Michael Berrow and arranged to meet Nick and Roger the following day.

"We knew instantly that he was the one," remembers Roger, and he made a deep impression on Nick:

"I liked his book cos it'd got nice drawings on the front, and he'd got the most ridiculous pink-spotted leopardskin punk trousers on, and sunglasses, so you couldn't see him at all. And a 1960s jacket. So I thought, anyone who looks that stupid and writes Rovostrov on the front of his exercise book is positively the one. He had this book which he was clutching very tightly and within the pages were written the first le Bon scrawls seen by man. And I was quite fascinated by how his mind worked, because he seemed to write about the most ridiculous things. I remember some of the titles that I read out of the book – 'On A Dead Child', 'Underneath The Clocktower' . . . one was called 'Night Boat' and another one 'The Chauffeur'."

No doubt unaware of the profound effect of his trousers, Simon also found the first meeting encouraging:

"*We seemed to get on very well actually, and they said come along tomorrow night, all the rest of the band will be here and we'll play a few numbers down. Having met Nick and Roger I thought, well, they have actually got some sense. They're not interested in doing it as a hobby, they think in professional terms. They think ambitiously and what I really want to do is get up on stage and perform, not train for it but actually do it.*"

So Simon went home, wrote some lyrics that he called 'The Sound Of Thunder', and went back the next night. The band played some of the numbers they'd been developing and, concentrating on one of them, Simon reworked his lyrics. Then he sang them and John remembers:

"*It was one of those magic moments. We were all playing and we looked round at each other and said, yeah, this is it.*"

Back side.

First photosession for EMI. Briefly considered as
cover shot for the first album. Milton Keynes,
February *1981*.

Front side. At Andy Earl's studio, Nottingham, February *1981*.

5

Early days. With Patti Bell of Kahn & Bell at the Rum Runner, December *1980*.

Parallel events had meanwhile been taking place in London. Former Rich Kids drummer Rusty Egan had been acting as DJ first at Billy's Club and later at the Blitz, his friend Steve Strange taking the cue from Studio 54 to keep a close watch on who came in at the door. Rusty played Kraftwerk, Bowie, Roxy Music, Nina Hagen, Talking Heads, Brian Eno to fashion-conscious crowds of young post-punkers, new-funksters and glam-rockers.

Others like Adam Ant and Toyah (both of whom were featured in Derek Jarman's punk film *Jubilee*) were developing their image in a similar direction. Chris Sullivan, Robert Elms and others were DJing and hosting their way to the front of an inspired and exciting new scene. Elms thought up a name for a band formed by friends: Spandau Ballet. Sullivan, Melissa Caplan, Jon 'Mole' Baker, Simon Withers, Willie Brown, Stephen Linard and Brummie Martin Degville were among young designers preparing their assault on the established world of fashion – some taking their cue from punk bondage, others from Bogart and zoot suits, still others from functional uniforms and Eastern European styles.

Japan's Roxy/Bowie influence was clear but they had not yet made any great impact at home. The Human League's synthesised tunes were beginning to seep through into the public consciousness. Similar clubs were springing up all over the country and the word was: **DANCE**.

Perry Haines had not yet used the description "new romantic" that was later pounced upon by a label-hungry press, but the feeling was already in the air.

Most of these scenes developed independently of each other. In Birmingham the 'posers', as they were called, went to Hawkins Wine Bar and the Hosteria in the evenings before going on to the Rum Runner or the Holy City Zoo. They bought their clothes at Kahn & Bell's in Hurst Street, who made and often inspired the transition from punk to punk-chic to poser. Local band Fashion were gearing up to yet another line-up change, founder members Jon Mulligan and Dik Davies ubiquitous members of the local scene.

For *Duran Duran*, the hardest bit was about to start. Simon still hadn't finally made up his mind to stay, but they worked hard over the summer and after spending a week together playing at the Edinburgh Festival, he decided:

"*Right, that's it, I'm going to drop out*

Birmingham, November *1980*.

of University. It was something we talked about. The whole band knew that I had to try it out for myself as much as they had to try me out."

The line-up was now complete. They had a unified notion of their music and they knew where they wanted to go: to the top. Paul and Michael officially became their managers. They wrote all their songs together and decided to split everything five ways, a fact that later protected them from many of the pressures and tensions that plague other bands.

Locally, they played the Holy City Zoo, the Cedar Club and, of course, the Rum Runner. In London, they played the Marquee (standing in for The Associates) and supported John Cooper Clarke and Pauline Murray at the Lyceum. But record company interest was still lukewarm, as Simon remembers:

"*We had two main ones lined up and they were a bit sort of, you know – there's lots of bands around at the moment, you have to try a bit harder, do a few more live*

shows, make another demo, that kind of thing. [So] we stopped bothering about record companies, we thought we'd get some live experience."

The 'live experience' they were looking for was the support slot on a major tour. They wanted to appear with an act that would pull in big crowds but had a sufficiently different appeal to emphasise their own personality as a band. The choice fell on Hazel O'Connor, who had just starred in the film 'Breaking Glass'.

Michael Berrow sold his house to raise the cash needed for the tour. Not that this yielded the trappings of stardom – they spent the entire tour living in a camping bus and they earned £10 a week each – but it made the next step possible.

"Hazel was very good to us on that tour," remembers Nick, "and that is where we really learned how to play live." The audience, recalls Simon, was quite tough – "a lot of punks and skinheads" – but the band made a sufficiently strong impression to arouse the record companies, three of whom were competing to sign them by the end of the tour.

One of the record company men who saw them on tour was Dave Ambrose from EMI.

Simon: "*He came on a couple of dates with us at the end. He just decided I suppose that we had the poke and the ambition to go through and make a good thing of it. So we stuck with him.*"

Duran Duran signed a worldwide recording deal with EMI Records within six months of their agreement with the Berrow brothers. They received a weekly retainer of £50 each – unheard of luxury. The pieces were in place; the band ready to show that all this confidence was not misplaced.

Faster than light. The first headlining tour, Birmingham, March *1981*.

Girls on Film.

On the set for the filming of **My Own Way.**

6

Between that day and this, **Duran Duran** have had seven hit singles and two bestselling albums. Their feet have hardly touched the ground since they started their first head-lining tour in February 1981. They've made ten videos (five in England, three in Sri Lanka and two in Antigua) and are in the process of completing a video album. They've done countless interviews and photosessions and have played live concerts in Australia, Japan, America, Canada, Sweden, Norway, Finland, Denmark, Germany, Holland, Belgium, France and Portugal.

Along the way they were dismissed by much of the established British rock press, dominated as it was by pseudopolitical hacks capable only of appreciating anguished cries from the oppressed, who saw the new genera-tion of musicians epitomised by **Duran Duran** as little more than clothes horses out to manufacture an artificial movement. Threatened by the lack of social messaging they needed to justify their existence as meaningful scribes, they resorted to flippant sniping at what they saw as nancy-boys in make-up playing catchy tunes without content.

The blinkered critics saw this union of rock and disco as a musical sin – what was there wasn't new, it was merely superficial. Behind their tut-tutting backs the fans were in at the birth of the love triplets: dance, power and atmosphere. It was irresistible pop with good songs and positive entertain-ment; before long, all that was left for the critics to do was regret the fact that the mixture worked.

"They may celebrate superficiality: they may be the kind of encouragement they think their pop can be. It's all so easy for them: how can anyone tell them it's not? They won't shorten anyone's life. In the face of darkness they glow and grin with a happi-ness lighting up the lives of the little girls." (*NME, July 1982.*)

If at first this disapproval was upsetting, they soon saw that the stamp of establishment favour isn't all it's cracked up to be.

Andy: *"I never ever want to be on the front cover of the NME. We would have given our left arm at one time for it, but now we'd never want that association. It's always good to have that negative element rubbing against your public, cos it winds fans up, it winds us up. And I love the way they think we're a pile of shits from Birming-ham. Great. They can leave it at that. It's*

not an honest sort of medium for us, cos we're nothing about what the NME is. We've nothing in common really, apart from it's supposed to be about music but it really has other radical ideas. We concentrate on making good records that we like. The whole thing has got to be there – the packaging, the quality, the class. We've never been into rip-ping people off. We've probably made less than any other new band over the past couple of years cos everything we make is just ploughed back in. It's honest to people. We get up on stage and play to each of them, it's that one-to-one thing with an audience. Musicians are about playing music to people, and the imagery and all the fancy of it."

To achieve the music, the imagery and all the fancy of it precisely as they wanted it, **Duran Duran** selected and worked with a variety of artists and craftsmen. Godley & Creme directed the video for 'Girls On Film'. Perry Haines, together with fellow i-D editor Terry Jones, directed the 'Careless Memories' video. But eventually it was Russell Mulcahey, who directed the Sri Lanka and Antigua videos, with whom they've built up a lasting and much stronger rapport. Other regular members of the team include Colin Thurston, their producer who has done much to help them develop their own distinctive recorded sound; graphic designer Malcolm Garrett; Alan Goldberg, who designs the stage sets and is in charge of lights; tour manager Richard Ames; booking agent Rob Hallett, who was recommended to them by UB40, ensures the tours are well planned; Neil Levine, out-front sound for live shows and Scottish Keith (Morris), on-stage sound; Mandy Berrow, wardrobe; roadies Chinese Rocks, Mick Hancock and Skal Loret; and much of their wardrobe these days is tailored in association with John Kaye, boss of South Molton Street couturiers Ebony.

When the first single was released, **Duran Duran** were probably the only one of the new generation to embrace the label 'New Romantic'. Most others – Spandau Ballet, the new Ultravox, Visage – refused to accept any tag at all and spent much energy denying the existence of a movement (thus giving rise to The Cult With No Name). To **Duran Duran** this did not matter. They *felt* like new romantics.

John: *"I think people always had the impression that we were a Foster Brothers version of PX; and we didn't go to the Beat Route every night. But looking back that was a good thing because it gave us our own headspace. Nobody's ever quite known what to make of us. They never really knew whether we were five polaroids that EMI had got together or whether we were the new Queen."*

Now they chuckle at those early shots with perhaps a hint of embarrassment, but it was a helpful stop along the way. As the band toured the world and created more music, its members started gaining the confidence to let their own personalities come through. If in

the early days the emphasis was on present-ing a cohesive image, it gradually became clear that the band functioned best when each member asserted his own personality – both musically and visually.

So from frilly shirts, via Antony Price suits and the affected, quasi-military veneer of the second British tour, **Duran Duran** arrived at what they see as a group of five honest, uninhibited individuals being them-selves.

Nick: *"It's just the way we are. I mean, Andy wears denim and leather jackets and jeans a lot and they suit him. And since we realised that, that we didn't all have to wear things that didn't suit us and try to be some-thing that we weren't, I think the image has improved greatly. And now it's really just five individuals."*

John: *"[For the second British tour] I'd gone for total white make-up and very deep lip gloss that matched my red hair. There was a Simon Fowler shot on the back of Smash Hits and I remember looking at it and saying, my God, what a bunch of tarts! But now we have nothing to be frightened of, nothing to hide. Now you're starting to see the real Duran Duran in the centre of Smash Hits, i.e. grinning inanely, wearing very casual clothes, which is really what we're all like as personalities."*

Destination – **Planet Earth.** Producer Colin Thurston at Chipping Norton Studios, *January 1981.*

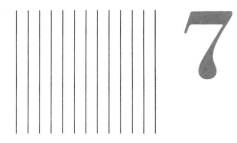

7

No sooner was the first single in the British charts than **Duran Duran** were already spending the proceeds on a massive programme of touring, recording and filming that keeps growing with every step. In the process, they have consolidated success at home and become massively popular in countries as far distant as New Zealand, Portugal and Thailand.

The three videos made in London for the singles off the first album – 'Planet Earth', 'Careless Memories' and 'Girls On Film' – gave them a taste for this medium which, though already widely used to promote singles, was rarely pursued seriously or consistently. Its potential was to give free rein to their imagination: they could be in a million places at once, evoke countless moods, construct storylines to complement the music.

Nick *"Video's great. I'm very interested in old films, adverts, television and video clips. I think it's a great medium and it's been good for us because within the next few years – time permitting – we would very much like to get involved with a feature film, and video helps you understand a lot about production, directing and filming. We view videos more as an artform; rather than banging out a promotional video, we try to put them together as we put our records together."*

One of the fundamental characteristics that makes **Duran Duran** what they are is the result of their early decision to write everything together, to split all the proceeds and to be equal members of the band.

John: *"We're one of the only bands where there's not one man who takes the credit. We've always been like a box of Quality Street: every one is someone's favourite . . ."*

Apart from forestalling resentment, this equality also ensured that each member pulled his weight. In theory each member writes the music for his own instrument – Simon writing both the lyrics and the vocal tune – but in practice the system is much more fluid, with each of them contributing ideas in the others' spheres. If in the first album they were still trying to emulate too many of their influences, the intensive touring, filming and writing that followed knocked them into their own shape.

John: *"We found our identity in such a short space of time. 'Rio' is probably the first real* **Duran Duran** *album, because it's honestly us, and it's us playing off each other. We'd gone through a lot of personality conflicts when we were doing 'Rio' because*

we were all growing up so much. We probably aged about five years in the last two cos things have moved so quickly. So 'Rio' was quite difficult cos we were niggling with each other and taking sides. But then when it was made we all sat there and we thought, well, we can argue all we like but musically it just hangs together perfectly. And then we say well, what the hell are we arguing about?"*

Nick: *"Tunes can come from anywhere really. An example is 'Hungry Like The Wolf'. I was in the studio with Simon one morning, we were really stuck for things to do, and I came up with a couple of chords that I quite liked and I carried on playing them, played them through on the synths for a while. Then Simon started humming along to it, liked it, and I changed one of the chords and the whole thing fitted together better. There was only the two of us in there so I put it down with a rhythm box and Andy came*

in. He listened to it and put a great guitar line on it which totally changed the whole face of it, it was starting to sound a lot more musical by then. Then Simon decided he'd got enough for the vocals, so he went and put a rough vocal on it. Then John and Rodge came in. Rodge overdubbed drums where the rhythm unit was, changed all the fills and sorted it all out properly. And John played in the studio off the monitors; his playing changed the face of it again, and it just all fitted together like a jigsaw. Then Simon scrubbed the vocal cos he'd written the words – and we had it finished in seven, eight hours at the most. But that's just one example of many ways things are written."*

The arguments rarely get out of hand.

Andy: *"The one surviving factor about us is that we don't take ourselves too seriously. Nobody gets really upset with anyone else . . . or listens!"*

Five fly to Paradise. Sri Lanka, April *1982*.

Licensed to Kill.

Phew, what a scorcher! D*urans* race for their shoes after a video take in which they solemnly endured the torture of having to stand barefoot on the hot stone floor of a Buddhist temple.

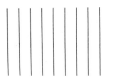

8

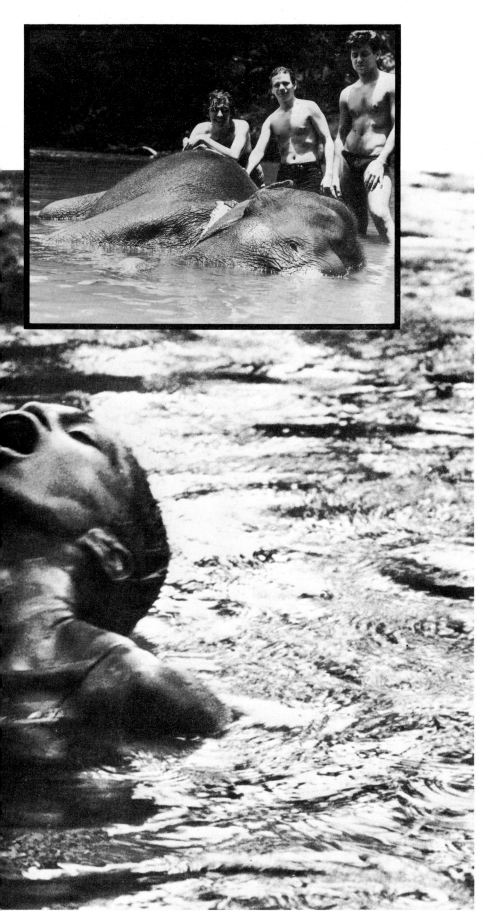

There are times when the whirlwind is more like a hurricane. When the band went to Sri Lanka to film the videos for 'Hungry Like The Wolf', 'Save A Prayer' and 'Lonely In Your Nightmare', Nick and Andy stayed behind to mix the new album and a live version of 'Careless Memories', catching about four hours' sleep a night to finish it in time. That done, they caught a plane out to Sri Lanka and arrived there only to go straight out on to the set for filming.

If the water was a bit dodgy and the food sometimes suspect, the scenery and sunsets in Sri Lanka were awe-inspiring. Tropical greenery, endless beaches, massive sculptures carved out of the mountainface, ancient Buddhist temples; all this mingled with helicopters, video cameras and all the other gadgetry that inevitably surrounds the Durans to create an atmosphere that 007 would have been proud of. On-screen they stared solemnly upwards in a Buddhist temple; off-screen they charged outside as soon as the take was finished because their bare feet were scorching. On-screen Roger sat manfully astride an elephant as it plodded through the wash; off-screen he held on for dear life when the elephant heard the replay and charged off in pursuit of what it thought were its mates. They got on well with the Sri Lankans, who probably shared the feeling that they were meeting exotic, unusual creatures.

Next stop Australia and the first completely sold-out tour. 'Planet Earth' had been number one there on the strength of the video and airplay alone and the Durans were mobbed nightly as they arrived at their triumphant gigs. They all loved the world tour.

Nick: "*It can be a lot of fun, cos you get to meet so many interesting people. And I really like talking to people. I spend all of my life talking to people actually. So it's a really interesting opportunity and on top of that there's still nothing better than to get in front of a crowd of people and perform the stuff you've written to a great reaction.*"

Andy: "*I'm thankful that I could even just go out there, go right round the other side of the world and see all that, which I'd never ever have done had I not been in the*

The British Tour, November *1982*.

All that glitters...

Setting the scene: *Duran Duran* with most of those who make up the regular team, photographed for *Smash Hits* centre spread. Hammersmith Odeon, London, November *1982.* **Key: 1.** Guest musician Andy Hamilton – saxophone, piano, percussion; **2.** Press Officer Suzi Rome; **3.** Driver/bodyguard Bosch; **4.** Dave Mills – backstage security; **5.** Fan Club secretary Koren Foxx; **6.** Wardrobe assistant Mandy Wallis; **7.** Wardrobe manageress Mandy Berrow, sister of Paul and Michael; **8.** Label manager David Hughes of EMI Records; **9.** Caroline Hood – secretary to David Hughes; **10.** Booking agent Rob Hallett; **11.** Kasper de Graaf; **12.** Malcolm Garrett; **13.** Manager Michael Berrow; **14.** Anne Williams; **15.** Tour Manager Richard Ames; **16.** Guitar roadie Skal Loret; **17.** Ian Ure; **18.** Keith Morris – on-stage sound; **19.** Iain Scott – sound system rigger for live shows; **20.** Adrian Carroll – lighting technician; **21.** Peter Long; **22.** Andy Beattie; **23.** Drums roadie Mick Hancock; **24.** Sound engineer Neil Levine; **25.** Lighting technician David Morphy; **26.** Lighting technician David Farmer; **27.** Set designer Alan Goldberg; **28.** Coach driver Steve Darrall; **29.** Sound system technician Zeb White; **30.** Wendy Germain – caterer; **31.** Val Bowes – caterer; **32.** Key-boards roadie Chinese Rocks; **33.** Merchandising agent Mike Smith; **34.** Truck driver Roger Mercer.

band. You think about people in a different way. Nobody seems like a foreigner because we go to so many places, it doesn't seem like it's a long way away and they've come from afar. Everyone just becomes people, it's great. MUSIC IS THE ONLY INTERNATIONAL LANGUAGE IN THE WORLD."

Duran Duran's technique of flying round the world all the time has proved to be the best way of keeping their feet on the ground, for it keeps them in touch with their audiences – and with each other.

John: *"It always helps when you're touring, cos when you do a good gig it brings you together like nothing on earth. You know, you come off and you go, yeah, weren't we great tonight? You can be number two in the charts and it doesn't make any difference, you can still have arguments over what you're doing. So you still need those reassurances from coming off stage."*

For Andy the hurricane had meanwhile developed into his very own private tornado. Work hard and play hard was his philosophy and he took both parts seriously, playing his gigs and then partying through the night. Whether it was a bug he picked up in Sri Lanka or his uncompromising lifestyle remains a matter of dispute between him and everybody else respectively, but at the end of the Australian tour he collapsed on stage and was unable to return for the final encore. He recovered sufficiently to do the tour of Japan (sufficiently, in fact, to become well acquainted with Tokyo's Lexington Queen and other glamorous nightspots) but paid for it when he finally returned home.

"We did Peter Powell's TV show Get Set For Summer *on the Saturday and on Sunday I went horseriding at one o'clock. By three o'clock I was in bed with a temperature of 104. Girlfriend [Tracey, now his wife] panicking away – cos she was ill as well, she had flu – and I'm sweating. I phoned up John and I went, can you get us a doctor? He says, what the . . . So I said, just send one. The doctor said, I think you've got malaria. Ee-aw-ee-aw, ambulance down. I was in for five days and they just cleaned me out."*

The setback caused the band to reschedule their European tour and Andy to take things at a (slightly) more reasonable pace when on tour.

Back in Japan they had learned more about the hazards of being pop stars. Again they were mobbed at the concerts and received a tumultuous welcome, but this time their hotels were constantly besieged by crowds of Japanese girls and whenever they went out they were followed by a posse of taxicabs. When John and Roger tried to be clever once, sneaking out to do some shopping on their own, the police had to close down the store they went to and escort them back. But all that was part of what they were there for and it was a price they happily paid.

The calmer beauty of the Carribean Leeward Island of Antigua was the setting for their next two videos: 'Rio' and 'Night Boat', the latter featuring particularly spooky guest apperances by manager Michael Berrow, and the band's personal looker-afterer, Simon Cook.

By now their relationship with video director Russell Mulcahey had developed into a fertile basis for their video ambitions. Production of the video album was put in hand, using the available **Duran Duran** videos as well as live and specially made footage.

From Antigua they hopped across to America for the start of a two-month tour of Canada and the USA, playing audiences ranging from 600 to 40,000. It was the second visit there and another stage in the effort to build a strong American following. It is traditionally the hardest market to conquer, mainly because radio stations are local and mostly very conservative. They made a host of appearances on radio and TV chat shows. They played their concerts and persuaded thousands more that **Duran Duran** make good music. Halfway through, Andy married Tracey in Los Angeles and all the band were there in top hat and tails – neatly groomed for their guitarist and the girl they'd all first met when she styled their hair at the Wilson, Wilson & Wilson salon in Wolverhampton. Then, for the second half of the tour, they gained maximum exposure by supporting Blondie – taking a leaf out of their own book to break America as they had Britain.

California wedding. Los Angeles, July 1982.

9

In more than seven months of virtually non-stop touring round the world from April to December 1982, only two significant upsets have occurred – in August when Andy collapsed, and in October when John injured his right hand in a Munich hotel. Both incidents affected dates in Western Europe, but neither brought them to a standstill for more than a few weeks. At the time of writing, **D**uran **D**uran are preparing for the climax of the World Tour 1982 – a British tour that includes six shows at London's Hammersmith Odeon and culminates as always at the home base in Birmingham, this time for five nights.

They show no sign of losing momentum or appetite. The crowds may be bigger, but they remain as eager to move on as they were at the outset.

Andy: *The novelty wears off very quickly about things. We record something, think it's great and three weeks later we think, God, I don't like that, next time . . . And if you haven't got that constant eagerness to change things, always to look ahead and rip your stuff to bits, to try and do better, then you'll just hit a point where you stop. But we're always analysing things.*

"If we'd ever got this far two years ago we would have been well pleased. But now . . . we haven't even started yet!"

The British Tour, November *1982.*

John Taylor with guest saxophonist Andy Hamilton. Hammersmith Odeon, London, November *1982.*

Steve Harley of Cockney Rebel joins the band on stage at the Hammersmith Odeon to sing with Simon in a cover version of Harley's 'Come Up And See Me (Make Me Smile)'. London, November *1982.*

BY NICK RHODES

MOTTO – *"Think Big" and "Legs are best"*

FILMS – *Tess; ET; Casablanca; Napoleon; Nosferatu; Niagara; Performance; Jason & The Argonauts; Cabaret; Un Chien Andalou; The Tenant; Eraserhead; Death In Venice; The Sound of Music; Gigi*

DIRECTORS – *Roman Polanski; Steven Spielberg; Nick Roeg; George Lucas*

TV – *Family Feud (NY); Arena (London); Don Laine (Sydney); Funky Tomato (Tokyo)*

LIKES – *Art; strawberries; animals; Roxy Music LPs; Berlin; synthesisers; glass; pussycats; legs; TV; ice; Dover Sole; NY; neon; video; JVC; Aston Martin; Dun Fey classics; leather; memorabilia; films; Nastassia Kinski; Italian Vogue; Ku; Nagel; magazines; Tony Bartender; Andy Taylor's sense of economics; yachts; trivia; Bollinger 75; English dailies; Ebony; Antony Price; YMO; 60s British films; sleeping; records; Skating Vicar; pretty faces; nostalgia; people; soul; buildings; pink flamingoes and black panters*

DISLIKES – *Dishonesty; heavy metal; watches; being sick; bad travel agents; cats eating birds; political rock magazines; copies; bigheads; reading maps; beans; language barriers; aeroplanes; green and orange; forgetting birthdays; falling off horses; business meetings*

ACTORS – *Dustin Hoffman; John Hurt*

ACTRESSES – *Sophia Loren; Nastassia Kinski*

TOOTHPASTE – *Colgate*

MUSIC – *Sinatra; Bowie; YMO; Talking Heads; Roxy; Film; Amanda Lear; Grace Jones; Bing; Eno*

MAGAZINES – *Italian Vogue; New Sounds New Styles; Zoom; Interview; Ritz; Smash Hits; Ibiza Nightlife; Tatler*

BOOK – *From A to B and Back Again – Andy Warhol*

HATS – *Captain Scarlet; Fedora; black leather cap*

PHOTOGRAPHY – *Dean Chamberlain; Babushkin; Helmut Newton*

HOTELS – *Ambassador East (Chicago); Chateau Marmont (LA); Sherry Netherlands (NY); Blakes (London); Kao Plaza (Tokyo); New Oriental (Gaul, Sri Lanka); Boulevard (Sydney)*

T-SHIRTS – *Andy Warhol's Bad; Pineapple Dance; St. Martins*

CITIES – *NY; Sydney; London; Rome; Paris; Geneva; Gaul; Chicago*

VEGETABLES – *Broccoli; potatoes; peas (frozen); carrots*

DRINKS – *Russian vodka; Krug; Bollinger 75; Screwdriver; Remy Martin; pink Gin; anything but Jack Daniels*

GAMES – *Pop Group; Monopoly; Scrabble; Chess; Cards; Tennis; Speculate; Mousetrap; Twister*

INSTRUMENTS PLAYED – *synth; guitar; triangle; TV; SX70; telephone; oboe*

FAVE WORDS & PHRASES – *Turgid; dilemma; sex; koala; benestrophe; "talented young man"; meow; beatnik; "good answer, good answer"; "bumble bee"; aroused*

NOT FAVE WORDS & PHRASES – *Taxi (tacksy); cake; "have a nice day"; potty; homogenous; pretzel; teeth; suffocate; congenial*

PREVIOUS HAIR COLOURS – *blonde; brown; black; pink and black; burgundy; red; orange; pink/blue/blonde; blonde and red; black and blonde; auburn; fire*

BREAKFAST – *Strawberries and Champagne*

BY *JOHN TAYLOR*

Section One: The Media

FILMS — *Performance; ET; all Connery 007s especially Goldfinger; Raiders Of The Lost Ark; The Apartment*

TV — *Thunderbirds; Fawlty Towers; The Saint; Saturday Nite Live; James Garner; Polaroid ads*

ACTORS — *Sean Connery; Jack Lemmon; Harrison Ford; Scott Tracey; Roger Moore*

ACTRESSES — *Faye Dunaway; Catherine Deneuve; Jane Fonda; Marilyn Monroe; Anita Pallenberg*

MUSIC — *ABC; New York Dolls; Robert Palmer; Bowie; and inevitably, Byron and the Roxy Doxies (from Vol. 1, Avalon)*

MAGAZINES — *Music Life (Japan); New Sounds New Styles (deceased); Oui (anywhere); Clic (Sweden); Smash Hits (UK); Harpers (for a laugh!)*

BOOKS — *Francesco Scavullo – Scavullo On Beauty; James Clavell – King Rat; Philip Norman – Shout; Helmut Newton – White Women; F. Scott Fitzgerald – The Last Tycoon; J. C. Suarez – Manhattan*

Section Two: The World

CITIES — *Sydney; Copenhagen; Toronto; Birmingham; Tokyo; Los Angeles*

NIGHTCLUBS — *Peppermint Lounge (NYC); Embassy (London); Lexington Queen (Tokyo); Channel One (Copenhagen); Bennys (Sydney); Rum Runner (Birmingham)*

FOOD — *China (Los Angeles); Clydes (Washington); Big Macs (anywhere); but nowhere to beat Jonathans (Brum)*

DRINKS — *Sambuka; Veuve Cliquot; Long Island iced tea; fresh orange juice; sake*

BREAKFAST — *English traditional, lime marmalade*

CIGARETTES — *Kent, preferably 100's, preferably giving up!*

CARS — *Cord; BMW; Porsche 948; black Golf TI and Mercedes Benz of any type!*

Section Three: Myself

LIKES — *Sun, sea, sand and piracy; Amanda Lear; the Rocker Brothers; leather*

DISLIKES — *Dishonesty; megalomania; arrogance*

INSTRUMENTS PLAYED — *primarily bass, but a bit of piano, guitar, synths, drums – anything you hit and don't blow!*

PERSONALITIES — *The Duranettes; Johnny Thunders; Simon G. Cook; Molly Meldrun; Kevin Turvey; Chinese Rocks; Bryan Ferry; Bob Hattersley; The Beatles; Mick Jagger*

WOMEN — *Rennee Rousseau; Tanya Roberts; Amanda Lear; Modesty Blaise; Silk Legs; Debbie Harry*

STYLE — *NOT this month's Vogue*

Simon & Rodge & Ronnie in L.A.

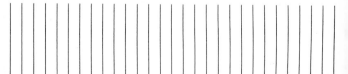

BY S*IMON le BON*

BIRTHDAY PARTY — *World of surprise, of fireworks and sudden silence. One moment half asleep in a stranger's bed the new day bursts in like a fast train or an old friend, ever expected but never knocking.*

FREE FALL — *A cold morning, a waste of snow and blue, nothing but a fast fading track of footsteps leading in one direction and a growing sense of purpose which points another way. All night parties, cocktail bars, the butterfly escapes the killing jar.*

EIGHT MILES HIGH — *The buds of cotton cloud buzz past the window like gunshots taken by the wind. One step farther, not one step beyond. Every second further away, another broken dream. Reality cracks and splinters before my face, falls like a shattered glass revealing that which I have always known; a portfolio of pictures I have never seen but know I must have drawn.*

THE SELF PORTRAIT — *Eastern jangles, flashes, jungles, all purple gold and red, a crimson flag to herald the dawn and from the centre of the liquid flame steps the man.*

THE UNION OF THE SNAKE — *Six foot deep the long night sleep and in my darkest hour, experience. The wakening. Within the man a dark uncoiling, the spring becomes a whip, thrashing upward, up toward ecstacy, up to break the sky, up to burn with the brilliance of lightning in secret Oktober.*

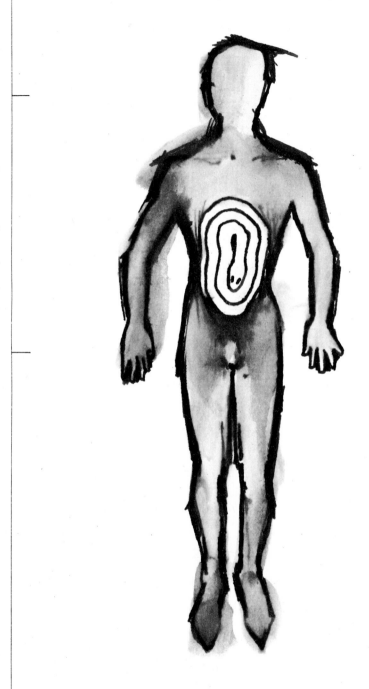

BY ANDY TAYLOR

MOTTO – *"You're a child genius"*

FILMS – *Raiders Of The Lost Ark; Blade Runner; ET; Author*

TV – *Crossroads; Basil Brush; Startrek; Blankety Blank*

LIKES – *Mom and dad; Tracey; Charlie dog; Bourbon; brandy; rock 'n' roll; loud guitars; lots of guitars; business meetings; royalties; my shoes; American TV; guns; Prince Charles; my sense of economics; horses; dogs; parrots; Guinness; sex; legs; excited audiences; obedience; bottoms; blonde screaming girls; blue eyes; Billy Wilson; bodyguards; going home; touring; afternoon tea; Earl Grey tea; twiddling knobs; food; pizza; dreaming; blues; money; comfort; work; bondage; accounts; banks; vitamin tablets; nice carpet*

DISLIKES – *Hangovers; pretence; bad organisation; cancelling tours; Paul Morley and the NME; dogs messing on the carpet; Sri Lankan germs; fascists; commies; aggro; breaking strings; losing money; flying; arty farty conversations; losing my temper*

SPORT – *Horse riding; tennis; throwing the javelin; basketball; cricket*

ACTORS – *Harrison Ford; Dustin Hoffman*

ACTRESSES – *Bo Derek; Stephanie Powers*

FOOT POWDER – *Scholl*

MUSIC – *Old jazz and blues; George Benson; Beatles; Stones; Clash; movie music*

AUTHOR – *Basil Ebury*

BOOKS – *Up the Organisation; Fair Stood the Wind for France*

SHOPS – *Head shops; delicatessens; Roche Borbois*

HOLIDAY RESORTS – *Lausanne (Switzerland); Copenhagen (Denmark); Los Angeles (USA); Antigua Island (Caribbean)*

FAVE CRISPS – *KP salt 'n' vinegar; chicken; prawn cocktail*

FOOD – *Italian (lots of garlic); pizza; English dinners*

DRINKS – *Milk; all sorts of teas; brandy; whiskey*

GAMES – *Chess; poker*

INSTRUMENTS PLAYED – *guitar; piano; flute; tabla; synthesiser*

TURN-OFFS – *Blood; fighting; puke; BO; dandruff; zits*

QUALIFICATIONS – *None*

HAIR HISTORY – *White; black; red; green; grey; yellow; orange; blue; Burgundy*

BREAKFASTS – *Scrambled eggs; toast; grapefruit; tea; milk*

LAST COMMENTS – *Don't believe everything you read in the newspapers*

Andy

Tracey

& Charlie dog.

BY ROGER TAYLOR

NICKNAME – *Froggy Barnacle* aka *The Frog*

INSTRUMENTS PLAYED – *Drums, congas, percussion*

MUSIC – *Peter Gabriel; Rick James; Roxy Music; Phil Collins; Donna Summer*

FILMS – *A Streetcar Named Desire; Casablanca; Poltergeist; Fun House; Some Like It Hot; On The Waterfront*

ACTORS – *Montgomery Clift; Jack Nicholson; Marlon Brando; Tony Curtis*

ACTRESSES – *Marlene Dietrich; Natalie Wood*

TV – *Wait Till Your Father Gets Home; The Adams Family; Bewitched*

MAGAZINES – *Smash Hits; Interview; Vogue; Zoom*

CAR – *Silver Porsche (Turbo 948)*

CITIES – *New York; Tokyo; Birmingham; Rome; Berlin*

CLUBS – *Lexington Queen (Tokyo); Heartbreak (NY); Rum Runner (Birmingham)*

LIKES – *Tony Curtis' haircut; the 40s, 50s and 60s; black-and-white movies; touring; my girlfriend; good food (especially French); sleeping in; good music; saunas; TV; sailing; dogs; playing drums*

DISLIKES – *science fiction; cats; being interviewed; people with bad manners; being unhealthy; going to the dentist; people who say "itsmorethanmejobsworthguv"; having no money; ignorance; flying; whiskey*

SHOES – *Black suede boots or Jazz shoes (preferably white)*

SOCKS – *White (always)*

HATS – *Baseball*

CLOTHES – *Baggy suits; blue jeans; T-shirts plus black leather*

DRINK – *Milk*

AMBITION – *Always to do something I love and to be remembered for having done something very well*

Andy with Eddie Van Halen at a Belgian TV studio.

DISCOGRAPHY

Albums

DURAN DURAN – EMC *3372*

Singles (7 inch)

PLANET EARTH/LATE BAR – EMI *5137*
CARELESS MEMORIES/KHANADA – EMI *5168*
GIRLS ON FILM/FASTER THAN LIGHT – EMI *5206*

Singles (12 inch)

PLANET EARTH (NIGHT VERSION)/PLANET EARTH + LATE BAR – *12 EMI 5137*
CARELESS MEMORIES/FAME + KHANADA – *12 EMI 5168*
GIRLS ON FILM/GIRLS ON FILM (INSTRUMENTAL) + FASTER THAN LIGHT – *12 EMI 5206*

This is a list of **D**uran **D**uran records as released in the United Kingdom; details vary in other parts of the world.

VIDEOGRAPHY

Title	Location
PLANET EARTH	St Johns Wood
CARELESS MEMORIES	Soho
GIRLS ON FILM	Shepperton Studios

RIO – EMC *3411*

MY OWN WAY/LIKE AN ANGEL – EMI *5254*
HUNGRY LIKE THE WOLF/CARELESS MEMORIES (LIVE VERSION) – EMI *5295*
SAVE A PRAYER/HOLD BACK THE RAIN (REMIX) – EMI *5327*
RIO/THE CHAUFFEUR (BLUE SILVER) – EMI *5346*

MY OWN WAY (NIGHT VERSION)/LIKE AN ANGEL + MY OWN WAY – 12 EMI *5254*
HUNGRY LIKE THE WOLF/CARELESS MEMORIES (LIVE VERSION) – 12 EMI *5295*
SAVE A PRAYER/HOLD BACK THE RAIN (12 inch REMIX) – 12 EMI *5327*
RIO (part 2)/RIO (part 1) + MY OWN WAY – 12 EMI *5346*

Title	Location
MY OWN WAY	St Johns Wood
HUNGRY LIKE THE WOLF	Sri Lanka
SAVE A PRAYER	Sri Lanka
RIO	Antigua
LONELY IN YOUR NIGHTMARE	Sri Lanka
NIGHT BOAT	Antigua
THE CHAUFFEUR	London

Three Duran Durans – *Andy Warhol.*
Studio installation, triptych. Artist's loft,
New York, August *1981.*

Nine Covers – *Duran Duran*.
Lithograph, Collection de Graaf/Garrett,
1981-82.

Smash HITS

35p USA #78
March 5-18 1981

15
HIT LYRICS
INCLUDING
DON'T GO
IT'S A MYSTERY
KIDS IN AMERICA
TALKING
HEADS

STRAY CATS
HONEY BANE

DURAN DURAN

Your Flexipop Flexi
the ASSOCIATES
Exclusive Track

FLEXIPOP!

Kim 4 Simon
true?
Le Bon meets La Wilde

MARI WILSON
TERRY HALL
MONSOON MARC ALMOND
IAN McCULLOCH

MADNESS
pin-up

NEW
SOUNDS
NEW
STYLES

NOVEMBER 1981 65p USA $2

GIANT
COLOUR POSTER

SOFT CELL
SIOUXSIE & BUDGIE
(SEE BACK COVER)

DURAN DURAN   MICHAEL JACKSON
HASLIN HAHN & BELL   SHOCK
ROBIN ONE   RICHARD BURGESS

SMASH HITS

38p APRIL 1-14 1982

SIMON LE BON
XTC·BAUHAUS·FASHION·EARTH WIND & FIRE
HAIRCUT 100·DOLLAR·U2 & MANY MORE
DEPECHE MODE·GENESIS IN COLOUR

POPPIX

NO. 10 60p
MONTHLY

DURAN DURAN   THE KIDS FROM FAME   JAM
FRIDA   DIRE STRAITS   DEPECHE MODE
KATE BUSH   HOT CLUB   WENDY WU

SEPTEMBER 11, 1982

CHARTBUSTERS

NUMBER TWENTY FOUR 65p

SPANDAU BALLET   TALK TALK
DURAN DURAN   MUSICAL YOUTH

SMASH HITS

38p AUGUST 19 SEPTEMBER 1 1982

DURAN DURAN
COOLING OFF IN CALIFORNIA
THE STRANGLERS
STING

HIT SONGS BY HAIRCUT ONE HUNDRED
HAYSI FANTAYZEE SURVIVOR AND MANY OTHERS
SIMPLE MINDS AND DONNA SUMMER IN COLOUR

THE LATEST CHARTS—AS USED ON TOP OF THE POPS

RECORD
MIRROR

DURAN
DURAN

The secret
diaries!

Dexys tour dates!

Junior live

Sheena Easton
Kate Bush LPs

David Essex

Boys Town Gang
Grand Master Flash

ABC   Haircut 100
Country fashions
for autumn

10 pages of hot colour!

NEW
SOUNDS
NEW
STYLES

JULY 1982 75p

DURAN DURAN
4-page pull-out feature

ABC

DAVID ESSEX QUINCY JONES
HAMMER HORRORS   THOMAS DOLBY
fashion: WITHERS / CHATTERS · TIN TIN